Another collection of Lyrical Riffs

More
Readings for Reflection,
Discussion and Worship

© 2018

i

For Marilyn,
Thank you for your encouragement
And for loving these readings.

List of Readings

1. Under the Radar
2. Light
3. When God Appeared
4. Refilling
5. Input
6. From the Heart
7. Your Song
8. One
9. For Those
10. You
11. Present
12. Happy Halloween
13. The Voice Cries Out
14. Want
15. Treasure
16. Be Still
17. Lifeblood
18. Graceland
19. Hashtags
20. You Cared
21. Fragile
22. Understanding
23. Small
24. The Embrace
25. This World
26. Sides
27. Bigger
28. Now

29. This Week
30. Seven days
31. These Hands
32. For Some
33. In Him
34. This Light
35. Honest to God
36. Depths
37. Safari
38. Tumbleweed
39. Stark Contrast
40. Natural Democracy
41. Someone in the Crowd
42. Signs
43. These Resurrection Days
44. The Revolution
45. In a World-Changing Week
46. Matter
47. To Know You
48. The Waiting
49. Control
50. Clouds
51. Us
52. The Greatest Story of Love
53. I Did This For You
54. Jesus Died for Them
55. Language
56. Circumstances
57. Wise
58. You Are There

59. Transfiguration
60. Help Us
61. Father Forgive
62. Recipe
63. Bread from Heaven
64. Nothing Off Limits
65. Psalm 1
66. Longings
67. Paving the Way
68. Promises
69. I Am
70. Open Book
71. The Whisper
72. Stumpery
73. Single Moment
74. Broken Praise
75. Searching
76. Don't Stop
77. Single Moment (2)
78. Present
79. Sour Wine
80. Carrying
81. Salvation
82. Carrying (2)
83. Living Sacrifices
84. No Longer
85. Longing
86. We Wonder
87. Filled
88. Christmas Everyday

89. Hallelujah, Amen
90. Sandals
91. Save Us/Holy Ground
92. Colours and Portraits
93. Daydream
94. Not Me
95. Dry and Dusty
96. Blunders
97. An Advent Prayer
98. Keeping Going
99. Changing Professions
100. Christmas Presence
101. New Year

1. Under the Radar

For a child is born to us,
So small, so frail, so vulnerable,
No fanfares or global advertising campaigns,
A quiet, subtle slipping into the world,
A new-born friend in the shadows.
A child is born to us,
In the darkness, in a strange place,
Under the radar,
The son of a powerless couple,
Found by inconsequential shepherds.
A child is born to us,
And we may often overlook him,
Sometimes forget the wonder
In the rush and the bother,
In the stress and the pressure.
A child is born to us,
And a man is on the way,
With hope in his hands,
Kindness in his smile,
Courage in his heart,
And the will to change everything.
For a child is born to us,
And thirty years of waiting begins.

2. Light

The people who walk in darkness
Have seen a great light.
So many of us need that light,
Glimpse it then lose sight again.
Need it to get through,
To keep going,
To know that Christmas is not merely
The glitter and shopping.
To know that this light is
Like no other,
To know that this light
Will lead somewhere.
So much darkness,
So much need of light,
And of strength and purpose,
Of healing and hope.
The people who walk in darkness
Have seen a great light,
A light that will shine on all
Who live in a land
Where death and despair,
Cynicism and blame,
Cast their long shadows.
The people who walk in darkness
Have seen a great light.

3. When God Appeared

When God appeared, they expected a warrior,
An angel of light, and a king.
Not a suffering servant, rejected and scorned –
No one expected him.

A fodder trough, a stable of pain,
A terrified mother-to-be.
Was this the man to change the world?
Was this the way to be free?

So he was born, in the dregs and the dung,
A fragile child of the night.
Outcast shepherds came to see,
And men from the East saw the light.

Yes, poor men and rich, were assembled that night.
Both wealth and poverty.
The kings brought gifts of spices and gold,
The shepherds just bowed the knee.

Is there sense in all this? Such a frail act of God,
Was their power in such poverty?
The search for the stable continues today,
There's a cross in its place – you can see…

That a man hangs in pain, nailed there with love,
And his mother's in agony too.
In the turmoil her mind drifts back to the stable –
Where she glimpsed what the future might do.

Gold for a king, incense for a God –
But myrrh, now that's for a cross.
And the king is enthroned with thorns and three nails;
And the God dies in frailty for us.

And Christmas is not just the snow and the glitter,
The turkey, the tinsel, the tree.
No – Christmas has come for the poor and the weak –
And it's here for you and for me.

4. Refilling

There's a hole in my soul
Where the hope leaks out,
Where the good intentions
Fall through.
Compassion escapes,
Strength ebbs away,
Meaning goes missing.
There's a hole in my soul,
Thank God for the One
With an unending supply,
Who is willing to keep on
Refilling.

5. Input

Earphones and Coffee Cups,
Input and sustenance,
Music and warmth,
Distraction and flavour,
Solitude and strength,
Word and spirit,
Love and life,
Giving and receiving,
Cross and resurrection,
One death,
For everyone,
Sustaining, reviving,
Inspiring, strengthening,
One Man,
For all.

6. From the Heart

Thank you that we can worship you
As we are,
No need for pretence,
Don't have to be good or look good
Or have all the answers.
No need to cover up,
Or say the right words,
Or hide from ourselves and you.
Don't need to use the right words,
Or know the right songs,
Or even sing in tune.
Thank you that we can come to you
As we are,
Any time of the day or night,
Any place in the world,
Any season of life.
Being honest and genuine,
Offloading our fears and troubles,
Because you understand
And you care.

Psalm 103

7. Your Song

Your song is eternal.
Not brash or abrasive,
Not self-seeking or proving a point,
Not a passing fad or fleeting trend.
Your song is stronger, gentler,
Kinder, more courageous,
Inclusive and welcoming,
And made of the smaller, precious,
Incomplete songs we offer to you.
You take what we have,
Arrange it, translate it,
Appreciate and treasure it.
Whatever the style or the volume,
The length or the eloquence.
You take our songs and make them yours.
And invite us to join you,
In that eternal, beautiful noise.
However we feel,
However competent we may be,
You call us out
To sing with you.

Ephesians 2 v 10

8. One

One group, one people, one body, one hope.
The struggling, the questioning,
The strong, the stable.
Those who know where they are going,
And those who don't,
Those who have answers and those who don't.
Those who dream, those who wonder,
Those who secretly limp,
Those who obviously meander.
Those we like, those we don't,
Those who help us, those who don't.
Those for whom each day is difficult,
Those for whom it is not.
The doers, the talkers, the achievers,
The befrienders, the listeners, the role models,
The smilers and frowners.
The ones who feel weak, and yet
Offer so much hope to others.
Me and you, them and us.
One group, one people, one body, one hope.

9. For Those

For those who find life hard,
For those who find faith hard,
Those who don't feel strong,
Those who don't feel powerful,
Those not sorted out,
Those for whom life is anything but tidy.
For those who feel as if they live in the dark,
Those who feel there's little or no light at the end of the tunnel,
Those for whom the way is often unclear,
Those for whom every road is full of twists and turns,
And the path is always uneven.
For those for whom life is not straightforward,
Yet courageously you keep going,
Your honest cry going up with every step.
As you place one foot in front of the other,
Grit your teeth and steel your nerves,
Those for whom life is a little easier
Send up small, heartfelt prayers,
As you share a glimpse,
Of Your long and difficult road.

'I am worn out, O Lord; have pity on me!
Give me strength; I am completely exhausted
and my whole being is deeply troubled.
How long, O Lord, will you wait to help me?'
Psalm 6 v 2-3

10. You
In the laughter and the longing
You are there,
In the deserts and the parties
You are there,
In the questions and the searching,
In the knowing and the unknowing
You are there.
In the smile of another
You are there,
In the small moments of hope
You are there,
In the reaching out to others
And the unseen acts of kindness
You are there.
In the now, in the present,
In this moment, in this reading
You are there.

Whether we are distracted,
Worried or tempted,
In the singing and the frowning,
Looking up or looking down
You are there.
In the crying and the honesty,
In the fear and covering up,
In the silence and the shouting,
In the gloom and in the wonder
You are there.
Though I may not be,
Though my mind may be elsewhere,

Though life's restlessness may trick me
And snatch me from this present moment,
Still you are there.
Here. Now. You. With us. With me.
Always.

11. Present

You are always present,
But I am not.
Often running ahead,
My mind elsewhere,
On the next thing,
And the thing after that.
Life's restlessness tricks me,
Takes me away from here and now,
Convinces me later is better.

12. Happy Halloween?

The light shines in the darkness,
Cloaked in pumpkin orange,
And cobweb grey.
Flickering tea lights peek from doorways,
Garnished with plastic skeletons,
Running with ketchup blood.
The darkness rises like a gloomy dawn,
Sending shudders through the lovers of light,
Putting the fresh rise of daybreak on hold.
Knock knock!
Who's there?
Famished treat hunters,
Hoping for a smile and a lot of sweets.
The light shines in the darkness
And the 31st of October cannot overcome it.

13. The Voice Cries Out

The voice cries out,
The voice of one calling in the wilderness:
'Prepare the way of the Lord, make his paths straight.'
Though our preparation may be small,
Our steps faltering and hesitant,
The path we follow rocky and winding.
Though we may not look impressive,
To ourselves or others.
The voice cries out, in whispers, smiles and sighs,
Calling in the streets and the shops,
In our houses and homes,
In our churches and cathedrals,
In our parks, cinemas and stadiums.
'Prepare the way of the Lord, make his paths straight.'
Inviting us to take time, pause, reflect,
To reconsider and see things a little more clearly,
Opening our eyes and softening our hearts,
Becoming aware of the ever-present God.

In the busyness and the pressure,
In the laziness and the leisure,
In the work, rest and play,
In the dark of night and the light of day,
The voice cries out, in whispers, smiles and sighs,
'Prepare the way of the Lord, make his paths straight.'
Whether we're peaceful, fearful or stressed,
Motivated, meandering or muddled,
Doing well, or losing our way,
Doubting, believing, questioning or convicted,
The voice cries out, in whispers, smiles and sighs,

For you and I, for them and us,
For the lonely and the popular,
For the young and the old,
For the well-off and the struggling.
The voice cries out,
The voice of one calling in the wilderness:
'Prepare the way of the Lord, make his paths straight.'

Luke 3 v 4

14. Want

I want to change the world if only I could,
Want to make things better as I feel I should,
Want to line things up the way that they should go,
Want to tell others to follow what I know.
Want to make things right, when so much seems so wrong,
Want to teach others to sing my kind of song.
But I can't do these things, my strength is not enough,
I can't walk this way – the road is far too tough,
But I can't stop wishing I could hold back the sea,
Can't stop willing others to change instead of me.
I know I need some help, someone to lift me up,
To help me glimpse the light when I want to give up.
And so I rest my head, lay my thoughts at the feet
Of one who knows and understands,
And has walked this weary street.

15. Treasure

Treasure in dark places,
Hidden, not from us, but hidden for us.
Treasure,
To find, to savour, to pass on.
Secreted in the darkness waiting for us,
Longing for our eyes to be opened and ears to be tuned.
Treasure,
Tiny precious discoveries,
As we walk, as we wait,
As we wander, as we work.
Treasure,
In the meeting of friends and strangers,
In sitting, standing, dawdling and slowing down,
Inside and out, around corners and in life's gaps,
Treasure,
In life's nooks and crannies and unexpected places.
Like a bright polished conker in a bed of mottled leaves,
A smile in a sea of disinterested faces,
A listening ear in a world of headphones,
A rainbow reflected in the mirror of a city puddle,
A gleaming white cross, jet trailed in a gloomy sky.
Treasure,
Waiting for us to look up,
Look around, look further and deeper,
Treasure,
Hiding, glistening, beckoning,
Twinkling at us, urging us to notice.
Treasure,
Whispering to us,
Offering us hope and a warmed heart,

Making us smile with its subtle, surprising hint of heaven.

Isaiah 45 v 3

16. Be Still

Be still.
Stop and listen.
For a moment... even... for 30 seconds,
for 20, 15, 10, 5...
Step aside from the rushing of your mind;
the scrambling of your day;
and the struggle of making life work.

Hear the shouts from the street,
the running of feet,
the voices you meet,
and the clock that we all try to beat.
Hear them... and leave them.
Remember... and let go.
Let go of all that clamours, all that crowds,
all that crashes in on the stillness of your soul.

Set these things to one side,
press the pause button,
for the shortest time.

And in letting go...
take the less familiar path that leads to those
mysterious still waters;
the peaceful brooks;
the cleansing streams.
Where a quiet calm sets aside, if only briefly,
the gasping of unsolved questions, and wearying
problems.

And as you approach those waters, drink of them.
If only the briefest of sips,
that you too may become for a moment... still...
and so become a fountain of life-giving water for others,
whether you are aware or unaware of this small miracle.

A subtle spring for those folks who
are still rushing,
scrambling and struggling
to make life work.

Psalm 23

17. Lifeblood

Dying to know us.
Dying to reach us.
Dying to nourish us.
Dying for a new life.
Dying for something better.
Dying for something real.
Dying for something genuine.
Dying for a fresh start.
Dying for a resurrection dawn.
Dying for everyone.
Dying for the lowest.
Dying for the highest.
Dying on a hill of forever.
Dying…
Yet living.
Blood shed…
For life.

18. Graceland

Imagine a land with no borders,
A place with no clenched fists,
A country where raised voices are a distant memory,
An open space bereft of slamming doors,
A forever kind of place.
Imagine a people with no prejudices,
No concern for pocket-lining,
No desire to slur or shame,
No knee-jerk reactions or road rage.
Imagine a time with no past or future,
Nothing to regret or fear,
No worries about other times,
No wish to flee the present moment.
Imagine a home full of welcome,
Saturated in loyalty and devotion,
Awash with encouragement,
In a land running with grace.

19. Hashtags

They call out –
Copy me
Like me
Follow me
Notice me.
Hashtags
Badges of hope.
We all wear them
To be liked
To be noticed
To be part of the crowd
To be popular.
The Ancient of Days put his hashtag on a hill
Stained red
Ragged and rejected
Tatty and torn
Shabby and shattered.
Yet people took notice
And still do –
Hashtagrescued
Hashtagvalued
Hashtagforgiven
Hashtagfreshstart
Hashtagpurposeandmeaning
HashtagtheGodwhodidn'tlooklikeanygodeverdidbefore
HashtagRagamuffinKing
Hashtaghope.

20. You cared

When no one else knew,
When no one else saw,
When no one else bothered,
You cared.
When no one else had time,
When no one else had strength,
When no one else had courage,
You cared.
When life was too busy,
When life was too distracting,
When life was too full,
You cared.
When I was frightened,
When I was alone,
When I was confused,
You cared.

When we were angry,
When we were frustrated,
When we were hitting out,
You cared.
When everyone was lost,
When everyone was struggling,
When everyone was sleepwalking into trouble,
You cared.
So much that you made it public,
So much that you made it permanent,
So much that you made it possible,
For us all.
For each one,

For the least
And the last,
You cared.

21. **Fragile**

Lord, we're so fragile,
Though we want to be so strong,
Want to be so right,
Though we often feel so wrong.
Want to walk with answers,
Though our hands are full of doubt,
Want to be successful,
Though we often flail about.
We come to you today,
Not a perfect offering,
But with all that we are,
With our flaws, regrets and failing.
Looking to the one who
Made himself fragile too,
As he sang his resurrection song,
So we could sing it too.
As he knelt in muck and grime,
Made himself so weak and wrong,
Did the wondrous work of change,
Knowing we were not that strong.

22. Understanding

Thank you, Lord, that you understand,
That you have lived this life,
Known sweat, tears, frustration and sadness,
Known wonder, laughter, satisfaction and joy.
You are not a God who has remained distant,
But one who has walked in this dust,
Felt the heat and cold of the world,
Warming and chilling your bones.
Thank you, Lord, that you understand,
You are a God who knows what it is to be human,
Having lived through childhood and teenage years,
Having worked and lived in oppressive times,
Having been misunderstood and celebrated,
Knowing what it is to have enough and to be empty,
Knowing love and loss, hate and rejection.
Thank you, Lord, that you understand,
That you are one who can help us,
Having drawn close, and knowing the ways of life,
Knowing us better than we know ourselves,
Understanding when we trip up yet again,
Saying and doing the wrong things,
The harmful things, the ridiculous things.
Thank you, Lord, that you understand,
And can help us.
So we take a moment now to come to you,
And offer all that we are... (pause)
In your precious name,
Amen.

Hebrews 4 vv 14-16

23. Small

When we look up at the night sky
And see the breath-taking work of your hands,
We wonder - what are people that you should care for us?
When we feel small and inadequate,
Powerless and easily swayed.
When we wish we could be heroes,
Yet find ourselves adrift in a sea of straying,
We wonder once again,
What are people that you should care for us?
When we find ourselves in a land of giants,
When others seem to ignore us,
Or disregard us, or let us down,
When we fail to make the kind of impact we long for,
We wonder once again,
What are people that you should care for us?
When we hear again that ancient story,
Truth and love pinned on a darkened skyline,
A kind courageous man held before us with three nails,
And we wonder why he would go so far for us,
We ask once again,
What are people that you should care for us?
We wonder again about that love,
The love so far beyond our understanding,
Bigger than our frequent mistakes and our little minds,
Small enough to reach into every crevice of our lives,
And we wonder once again,
What are we that you should care for us?

24. The Embrace

Unfailing truth and love have met together,
Righteousness and peace can be seen embracing,
Truth springs up from the earth,
And justice smiles down from heaven.
Like long lost lovers turning a corner,
And bumping into one another,
Truth and love cannot hold back
From that warm embrace;
That kiss that makes them inseparable.
Forever together now,
Forged on a hillside,
Written in blood,
And sealed on a sun-soaked Sunday morning.
As those two bits of wood arose,
That ugly moment of beauty,
Justice and mercy took hands
And heaven's heart broke into a million pieces.
And as dawn broke and the pieces reformed
Into a whole new creation,
Righteousness smiled from heaven,
And kindness and integrity
Kissed once more.
Sealing the agreement for all time.
For the universe. For you. For us.

Psalm 85 vv 10-11

25. This World
This world moves us
And shakes us,
Frustrates and makes us
Angry, livid sometimes…
The misjustice, the crimes,
Giving us such indigestible questions,
A kind of soulful indigestion.

How much more must it move you
And shake you?
Frustrate and make you
Angry? Livid sometimes.
The misjustice and crimes
Giving you such turbulent questions,
That age-old soulful indigestion.

If it makes us fume and huff,
Makes us feel like
We've had enough,
Makes us cry and wonder
And long to rip things asunder…

How much more do you fume and huff?
Are you made to feel like
Enough is enough?

Do you cry and wonder?
Longing to tear the sky asunder?

One thing we do know

Is that seeing this pitiful show,
You chose to risk it all, to embark upon
A trip between your world and this one.
Sailed oceans of struggle and time,
Made for Golgotha and started that climb
Which led to a humble, blood-stained cross,
You accepted the trauma of pain, death and loss.
Sinking so desperately, so miserably low,
As dark and as a lost as a person can go.
In order to reach for a whole other dawn,
A reversal of time and a resurrection morn.

And that rainbow promise
So etched in the sky,
Appearing when the blue
Waves the grey goodbye,
Now makes us think of a man
Strung up high,
And your plan to completely immerse yourself,
Within a world unable to help itself.

26. Sides
We so easily grab hold of God
And claim him for our side,
We're the ones in the right,
He's bound to be with us.
Yet forget the vital issue,
The question in the air,
What about us?
Whose side are we on?

27. Bigger
Love is bigger than anything
That might stand in its way;
A Roman cross,
A death penalty,
An angry mob,
A wall of prejudice,
Years of sadness,
A wave of cynicism,
A sea of despair,
An ocean of put-downs.

Nothing can step between us
And the greatest Love of all,
The kindest, smallest, gentlest,
Most powerful, courageous, profound,
The simplest, purest, smartest,
Undiluted Love of another world.
Another time, another dimension,
Another way, another heart.
Good, caring, patient, strong:
Another Father.

28. Now
He won't fix all your problems,
Though he may fix some.
He won't heal all your ills,
Though he may heal some.
He won't make everything easy,
Though some things may change.
He won't make you rich and famous,
He has other priorities.
But he is always there,
In the good times and bad,
Alive and unique.
Not a 2-dimensional cut-out,
Not a spiritual guru,
Not merely a pick-n-mix panacea,
Not simply one among many.
But unique and alive,
The bottom line,
Holy and accessible,
Kind and courageous.
Here.
With us.
With you and me.
Now.

29. This Week

This week
I will no doubt trip up.
Several times.
Fall on my face and look a fool.
I'll put my feet in my mouth no doubt,
Step in something inadvisable,
Reveal my fractured nature in a public place.
I won't appear all that successful
Or triumphant at times,
I'll not be flavour of the month,
Or the minute,
Or hero of the week.
I'll most likely be a loser from time to time,
Perhaps even topping the chart of losers.
And yet,
I'll still
Be loved.
By the Lover who doesn't expect
Our perfection.
He just invites
Our attention
And our bumbling friendship.

30. Seven Days

On the first day
God made a table and it was good.
On day two
God made four chairs, and these were good.
On the third day
God made a new start for some surprised disciples,
And he saw that this was good.
On day four
He made a sick woman well,
And this was very good.
On the fifth day
He made friends with a group of children
And breathed life into a dead man.
And this was also very good.
On day six
He took three nails and built a new reality
And this was extraordinarily good.
On the seventh day he walked out of a grave
And came to rest in a garden.
And it was perfect.

31. These Hands

This hand, an unknown woman, reaching up,
A lunge, a grab for the very edge of a cloak,
Healing, hope, desperation for a dying life.
A hand going down in history.
This hand, an unknown friend, reaching down,
A hole in a roof, lowering rope burning against skin,
Help for an injured man, a plea for a new start.
A hand going down in history.
This hand, an unknown soldier, reaching up,
A mottled sponge on a stained stick,
Vinegar, cheap wine, a drink for a dying man.
A hand going down in history.
Two hands, we're getting to know, stretched out,
Shaping the world from scratch,
Tortured, torn, hammered, laid bare for that very universe.
Two hands going down in history.
Our hands, as much as we know of ourselves,
Offered in ragged prayer, as much as we dare admit,
The good things, the bad, the hurting and hopeful.
Our hands, bringing our history, to his.

32. For Some
'I am with you always.'
For some it means putting one foot in front of another
For some it means getting through the nights
For some it means adventure
For some it means sacrifice
For some it means scaling walls
For some it means the strength to live with them
For some it means changing the world
For some it means coping and getting by
For some it means grabbing life with both hands
For some it means hanging on by their fingernails
For some it means all of the above
For some it means other things entirely.
How about you?
'I am with you always.'

Matthew 28 v 20, John 14 vv 18-19, Hebrews 11 vv 31-38

33. In Him

In him we live and move and have our being.
In him we wake and sleep, work and rest,
In him we eat and drink, give and take,
In him we smile and laugh, worry and weep.
In him we trust and doubt, question and rage,
In him we wonder and imagine, dismantle and create.
In him we meet others, friends, enemies and strangers,
In him we sing and dance, run and walk,
In him we rush and chase our tails,
In him we stop and quieten all that frets with in us.
In him we exist, with all that we like and dislike,
In him we are all that we are, and do all that we do,
In him we live and move and have our being.

Acts 17 vv 27-28 & Psalm 139 vv 1-18

34. This Light

The darkness can never overcome it,
This light, this love stronger than death,
Shines on in the shadows and the emptiness.
More resilient than doubts and despair,
Pressure and put-downs.
More present than the air we breathe,
Or the noise we make,
Or the sound of silence.
The darkness can never overcome it,
This light, this love stronger than death,
Shines on in the gloom and the night,
More present than we can know,
More than we can feel, sense or touch,
More than we can see or visualise.
Sometimes so evident to us,
Sometimes we strain for a glimpse, or a clue.
The darkness can never overcome it,
This light, this love stronger than death,
Shines on in the cynicism and distrust.
Not reliant on our strength, or our ability,
Our religious ways, or our goodness.
The darkness can never overcome it,
This light, this love stronger than death,
Shines on in the darkness,
In the day and the night,
In the past, the present and the future.
This love shines on.

35. Honest to God

Thank you Lord that we can be honest with you,
That we don't have to wear the masks we feel we must wear in life.
Thank you that nothing will shock you,
That we needn't put on the guise of strength when we are really weak,
That we need not wear success, when we have failed again.
Thank you that you understand the languages
Of loss and disappointment, failure and fragility,
Thank you that you deal in fresh starts,
Understanding the brightest of lights and the grimmest of nights.
The Good Shepherd not afraid to get his hands dirty
In order to help the sheep.

36. Depths

Out of the depths I cry to you, O Lord.
You know what it is to be hurting
Lord, hear my voice!
Let your ears be attentive
To the voice of my supplications!
Lord, you know what pain is like,
You know the deepest sorrow.
If you, O Lord, should mark iniquities,
Who could stand?
We cannot save ourselves, but you know that.
You know we are lost without you.
But there is forgiveness with you,
So that you may be revered.
You have made a way, walked in our shoes.
Taken our place.
I wait for the Lord, my soul waits,
And in his word I hope;
Waiting is not easy Lord, we live in a quick fix age.
Help us when our patience runs out.
My soul waits for the Lord
More than those who watch for the morning.
We are here now, calling to you,
Looking to you for strength, comfort and hope.
O Israel, hope in the Lord!
For with the Lord there is steadfast love,
And with him is great power to redeem.
You alone are Lord. We know that,
And you have the power to make all things new.
It is you who will redeem Israel from all its iniquities.
You can save us, you can help, you can make a way,

And give us a future and a hope.
We look to you, O Lord.
Amen

37. Safari

We like to think we know,
Like to claim we have it all worked out,
Tidy, measured, quantified, sorted.
But the invitation is to follow, to make a start.
Not to size it all up and stuff it in the right box.
But to walk in the steps of a man who knew conflict.
A man who knew sorrow, laughter, struggle and hope.
A man who set out on a safari through childhood,
Adolescence, young adulthood, school and work.
A safari of stories, dull days and extraordinary happenings,
Conversations, adventure, normality and relationships,
Bread, fish, wine and parties.
A safari through a country that would offer applause,
Banter, argument, arrest, death and resurrection.
A safari littered with footprints and invitations.
We like to think we know,
Like to claim we have it all worked out.
But the safari lies before us,
And we are taking a few steps each day.
And He is with us
Each step along the way.

38. Tumbleweed

Hosea, that old, old prophet, made a promise way back,
And Jesus knew it from his scraggy, ragged wilderness days.
The tender voice of God.
Tugging, sustaining, wooing, shaking, calming, supplying.
'I will lead my people into the desert,
And there I will speak tenderly to them.'
Deserts? Hmm… but tenderness…
Jesus sought out the dry places,
The barren lands of morning,
Went searching for the tender voice of his Father.
'This is my precious son, listen to him.'
'You are my precious child, treasured and valued.'
'I love you, let me see you and hear you.'
The tender voice calls, wooing, tugging, drawing, calming.
As life's tumbleweed skitters by.

Hosea 2 v 14, Song of Songs 2 v 14

39. Stark Contrast

Lord, we long to be strong,
To be impressive and powerful,
To be the greatest, the best,
The last one standing.
We forget that, in bloodied weakness,
In stark contrast to the earthly empires
Of might and pride,
You changed everything.
Not looking right,
To a world so wrong,
Yet being everything needed,
And all that was required,
To help us begin again,
To open the door that no one could close.
So today,
If we cannot be strong,
Impressive and powerful,
Be with us in our stumbling,
In our foolishness and mistakes,
And may our small lives be to you,
A vehicle for worship,
And a channel for hope.
Amen.

40. Natural Democracy
Isn't life a natural democracy?
Where we could be heroes and holy fools?
A place crafted free of tyranny,
Of oppressive leaders and twisted rules.

Isn't life a natural democracy?
Before peer pressure hems us in?
Before snags, slurs and wagging fingers
Turn us into a flat-pack being?

Isn't life a natural democracy?
Each born with a vital design?
No one slotted together from an Airfix kit,
The mould broken each and every time.

Isn't life a natural democracy?
Weren't we wired up at the start?
Carefully crafted by the Designer's hand,
Each life a piece of original art.

Isn't life a natural democracy?
Each crafted by the Caring hand,
To live unique, original lives,
The way only we can?

Psalm 139

41. Someone In the Crowd

Someone in the crowd,
So many times we feel the noise is just too loud,
Life's pressures and the clamouring of sound,
Drown out the one voice who can make us feel so much more
Than just someone in the crowd.

Someone in the crowd,
With the painted masks we so regularly wear,
And the faces we so lovingly prepare,
The rocks we hide behind and the fig leaves we do not dare
Let go of, because it's too risky to be found.

Someone in the crowd,
Cries for peace and love yet does not make a sound,
The longings hidden so that they might not be found.
We dare not show that we are weak and often cowed,
And so we wear the clothes of someone strong and proud.
Blending in so we're like someone in the crowd.

Someone in the crowd
Looks so normal, like he's merely hanging round,
Became one of us that we might each be found,
In the Easter love he lived and the life he spread around,
The brightest ever son, looking so much like any other one,
Just like someone in the crowd.

42. Signs
Those places that we love,
Those glimpses ever sweet,
The travelling which warms our hearts,
The best food we can eat.
Signs of You. Signs of Another World.

The calming moments of peace,
The promise of a better day,
Satisfaction and tranquillity,
Another place, another way.
Signs of You. Signs of Another World.

The longing for a better life,
The wonder of a child born,
The desire for truth and justice,
The dreaming of a brand-new dawn.
Signs of You. Signs of Another World.

The quest for hope and love,
The fight to put things right,
The breaking down of barriers,
The breaking through of light.
Signs of You. Signs of Another World.

Things that point to something else,
To another kind of birth,
A lasting kingdom, peace, shalom,
An Eden world, a revamped earth.
Signs of You. Signs of Another World.

Revelation 21 vv 1-4, Isiah 65 vv 17-25

43. These Resurrection Days

Joseph met his brothers, in Egyptian clothes and hair,
After years of separation they could not see him there.
He took the chance to trick them, set some traps along the way,
To see if they had changed, since that brother-selling day.
Two on a road and seven on the sea,
Bumped into a stranger, looking just like you or me.
Couldn't see him there, the one who turned back time,
Spent his life living for others and dying for our crime.
Mary in a garden, standing near a grave,
Could only see a gardener, not a man who'd come to save.
Not always easy to see you, in these resurrection days,
To sense you close to us, through life's distracting haze.
But you will never trick us, or lead us astray,
So Lord, please,
Quicken our senses to your presence with us today.

44. The Revolution

The Revolution will not be about fists and fury,
The Revolution will not be about bullying and bullets,
The Revolution will not be about hate and hurting others,
The Revolution will not be about revenge and retribution.
It will be shot through with patience and peace-making,
Kindness and compassion,
Courage and crossing divides,
Sacrifice and salvation.
The Revolution will not be so much glamorous as gutsy,
Not so much about putting on a show as putting aside egos.
It will continue quietly,
Noticed or unnoticed,
At work in the Lost Places,
And in the lives of the Lovers.

1 Corinthians 13

45. In a World-Changing Week

In a world-changing week,
Unafraid of humility and kindness,
The king rides in, looking small and vulnerable,
Coming so close, to see us and know us.
In a world-changing week,
Unafraid of humility and kindness,
The king gets his hands dirty, doing the job of a servant,
He kneels in the dirt and washes our battered feet.
In a world-changing week,
Unafraid of humility and kindness,
The king steps into the sad temples we build,
Tipping over the tables of our misplaced ambitions and hopes.
In a world-changing week,
Unafraid of humility and kindness,
The king volunteers and takes another's place,
Offers himself, for one and for all.
In a world-changing week,
Unafraid of humility and kindness,
The king refuses to lie still in a stone-cold tomb,
Dead yes, but then stirring once more,
Breaking death's dark conventions,
Battering down that door.
In a world-changing week,
Unafraid of humility and kindness,
The king waits to be seen, in a garden, on a road, by the shore,
Waiting still, for that pause in our busy lives,
For that moment of truth, when the stone roles from our eyes,
And resurrection wakes us one more.

46. Matter

You Matter.
Though circumstances may rail against you,
Though people may press you into a corner,
You Matter.
Though life squares up to you with the gloves off,
Though success eludes you,
Though your plans lie in tatters,
You Matter.
Because you are made of precious Godly dust,
Formed in the secret places,
Created, not thrown together by happenstance,
You Matter.
You really do.
You're a chip off the ancient block.
Made in the Creator's image,
No accident.
And no words, lawsuits, libel or accusations,
Can ever take that away from you.

Psalm 139

47. To Know You

More than just words on a page,
Or prayers in a service.
More than notions of belief,
Or rules and theology.
More than a hopeful solution,
Or a different world-view.
Beyond all this,
Richer than all this,
To know you.
To sense your presence,
To realise how much you value,
And understand,
Us,
As we do our best,
To value and understand.
You.
To know you.
In the rush and the panic,
The worrying and the fretting,
In the peace and the calm,
In the happiness and wonder.
To know you.
The quest goes on,
Catching glimpses here and there,
Our spirits quickened,
From time to time.
To know you.
That's our longing.

48. The Waiting

The waiting.
It seems to achieve so little.
The wandering, meandering days,
Each step weighing a little heavy,
And not necessarily in the right direction.
The waiting.
It goes on, and at times he is itching to start,
To begin doing worthwhile things,
Making a change, making an impact,
It's not easy.
The waiting.
There is so much to be done,
So little time,
And yet he is here,
Away from the action.
The waiting.
He could do a million things,
Concoct a world of good ideas,
Prove himself,
Make his point.
The waiting.
He feels the warmth on his face,
Senses within his being,
The unseen work of God,
Like stepping into sunlight,
Absorbing the ways of his father,
In the waiting.

49. Control

So tiring at times,
So wearing,
To hold those reigns,
Gripping so tightly,
Doing our best to keep hold
Of so many loose ends.
So difficult to let go,
So fearful… the prospect,
So stressful… the unknown,
So taxing… the holding on.
To begin again,
To step into the sunlight,
To breathe once more,
To stretch our spirits.
'Be still.'
The whisper in the air,
Even for a moment,
The gentle call,
To open those fists,
Unclench those hands,
And regain perspective.

50. Clouds

I watch the casually drifting clouds,
Making their gentle way across the blotting paper sky,
No rush hour for them,
No pressured race to get from A to B,
No traffic jam or clock watching,
Or lurking deadlines.
Definitely going somewhere,
But in no desperate hurry.
And I'm reminded of the slow moving
Work of God in our lives.
I want to rush it at times,
To get results,
To feel the surge of success,
To match up to the standards I set for myself.
But God is not a business manager,
Or a fitness trainer,
Or a quality control inspector.
And what he considers achievement,
Is not what others might consider to be so.
Winning, triumph and glory
Are another story to him.
And with glorious irony
Just stopping to watch these trundling clouds,
Slows me down and
Makes me pause and appreciate
The One who made them.

51. Us

We fear, We trust,
We laugh, We play,
We cry, We worry,
We work, We spend,
We doubt, We believe,
We sing, We question,
We agree, We argue,
We're frustrated,
And frustrating.
We sleep, We lie awake,
We watch, We listen,
We hope, We waiver,
We learn, We struggle,
We love, We pretend,
We tell the truth,
We don't.
We like each other,
We don't like each other,
We're strong, We're weak,
We wait, We're impatient,
We're weary and restless,
We behave and misbehave,
We need
Him.

52. The Greatest Story of Love
The Greatest Story of Love,
Of courage and kindness,
Purpose and meaning.
The Greatest Story of Love,
Accessible to all,
Available free of charge.
The Greatest Story of Love,
Of a man bursting out of water,
The sun reflected in the drops,
And his father's voice ringing in the sky.
The Greatest Story of Love:
'This is my son, listen to him.'
And for us, for you and I, for all of creation,
He steps into the dry and dusty wilderness.
The Greatest Story of Love:
So begins his journey,
Through miracles and conflict,
Courage and kindness.
The Greatest Story of Love,
Set high upon a cross,
Dying and living again,
Offering everything he has,
Saying, 'Take a step, begin again.
See where this road leads.'
The Greatest Story of Love.

53. I Did This For You

I was born in poverty,
Lived in a corrupt place;
Wandered without a home -
Misunderstood by my family.
I was deserted by friends,
Rejected by the religious
And betrayed by a disciple.

I was mocked by hypocrites,
Condemned in fear;
Beaten by thugs
And stripped by thieves.
Tortured for sport,
Hammered to a cross.
I died in agony
And was buried in someone else's grave.

I did this for the world,
For all of creation,
For my friends and my enemies,
For the old and the young,
The captives and the free,
The weak and the strong,
I did this for you...

54. Jesus Died For Them

Judas betrayed Jesus
Peter denied Jesus
Thomas doubted Jesus
Jesus died for them.

Pilate rejected Jesus
Herod taunted Jesus
Caiaphas framed Jesus
Jesus died for them.

The soldiers crucified Jesus
The disciples deserted Jesus
The people laughed at Jesus
Jesus died for them.

Mary wept for Jesus
The women anointed Jesus
Joseph buried Jesus
Jesus rose for them.

We have doubted Jesus
We have denied Jesus
We rejected Jesus
But Jesus died for us.

55. Language

The first language of God is silence.
Not success,
Or victory,
Or popularity,
Or power.

The first language of God is silence.
Not a clamouring,
Or a shouting,
A vying for attention,
Or a desperate plea to be picked.

The first language of God is silence.
Though we may wish otherwise,
Long for a dramatic monologue,
Or a tender whisper.

Instead…
The silence of a corpse on a cross,
And a pre-resurrection tomb.
The silence of a lone figure in the wilderness,
A rabbi praying in the early morning,
And a creation waiting for that first stirring word.
In the quiet of every moment when
You and I think that nothing is going on…
The first language of God is silence.

56. Circumstances

To know you in all circumstances…
Not necessarily as an escape or a panacea,
Or perhaps as an excuse or explanation,
But as a God who has promised to be with us,
And has lived all the circumstances.
Knows the struggle and the joy,
The pain and the frustration,
The questions and the silence,
The laughter and the liking.
The noise and bustle and distraction,
The wonder and the woe,
The money and the lack of it,
The loneliness and the friendships.
To know you in all circumstances…
To get that nudge,
That sense,
That you are there
With us.
Understanding.
Present.
Making that difference,
However small or large.

57. Wise
Wise folk out shopping,
Browsing the markets and shelves,
Looking for the ideal gift,
For a new born king.

Wise folk wondering,
What will sum up,
A life written in the stars?
An everlasting reign.

Wise folk surprised,
By the prompting they sense,
Among the bustle of ordinariness,
And the hustle of life.

Wise presents of regal Gold,
Divine Frankincense,
And anointing Myrrh.
Really? For a tiny, bright-faced child?

Wise people still wonder,
As they travel life's dusty streets,
What they might bring,
To the tiny child who grew up?

Wise folk still surprised,
That the best thing they can offer to
The one who has everything,
Is themselves, and their tumbledown lives.

58. You Are There

In the first waking moments as we enter this world,
You are there.
In our growing and discovering,
You are there.
In our learning and questioning, arguing and boundary pushing,
You are there.
In our dreaming and planning, hoping and scheming,
You are there.
As we get things right and wrong, as we triumph and stumble,
You are there.
Minute by minute, day by day,
Sometimes tangible, sometimes not,
In our trusting and doubting, praying and ignoring,
As we laugh and banter, shed tears and sweat,
You are there,
In the seconds and the hours, the years and the decades,
In our first hellos and final goodbyes,
You are there.

59. Transfiguration

Lord, you changed that day,
Transfigured those moments,
Brought glory to that mountain top,
Right into the lives of those everyday disciples.

Lord, as we continue through this day,
This week, this month, this year,
Help us please, to catch those glimpses of transfiguration.
Those moments of your glory,
Your presence, your light,
Shining in the everyday;
Breaking into our lives again,
Reminding us that you are no ordinary God,
And that you are with us -
The God of light, the God of hope,
The God of transfiguration.

60. Help Us

When we are tempted to put others down
Help us to overcome evil with good
When we long to pass on the latest piece of gossip
Help us to overcome evil with good
When we want to push others away
Help us to overcome evil with good
When we are invited to nurture negative attitudes
Help us to overcome evil with good
When cynicism is the easy option
Help us to overcome evil with good
And when we hear your gentle voice calling us towards love
Help us to take note and respond
In Jesus name
Amen

Romans 12 v 21

61. Father Forgive

Father forgive them for they don't know what they are doing.
Thank you so much Jesus, for those words of forgiveness.
Thank you for the releasing power of your sacrifice on that cross.
Father forgive them for they don't know what they are doing.
Lord please help us with our relationships,
Help us when it's difficult, when things go wrong.
Father forgive them for they don't know what they are doing.
Please help us to have the courage and the gentleness
To relate to one another about past mistakes
And those things that have hurt us.
Father forgive them for they don't know what they are doing.
Thank you for your forgiveness,
And for the new start you have given us,
Thank you for the chance to begin again.
Father forgive them for they don't know what they are doing.
Please help us, not just today, but in the coming days,
To weave honesty, integrity, forgiveness and truth,
Into our daily lives and relationships.
In the name of Jesus we ask this,
Amen.

62. Recipe

A sprinkling of compassion,
A cupful of kindness,
A pinch of diligence,
A handful of hope.
A spoon of perseverance,
As much patience as required,
A smattering of integrity,
A bucket of courage.
Mix sensitively
With the Spirit of God,
Wait a while,
And see what comes out.

Colossians 3 v 12

63. Bread from Heaven

As they were crossing the wilderness to the
Promised Land the people cried out to Moses for food.
Then the Lord said to Moses, 'I am going to rain
bread from heaven for you, and each day the people
shall go out and gather enough for that day.
In that way I will test them, whether they will
follow my instruction or not...'
We call out to you now, our precious Lord,
For the things we need,
Today, tomorrow, and in the week ahead.
God's mercies are new every morning,
great is his faithfulness...
We look to you, Lord, for help and provision.
Man shall not live by bread alone...
You fed the people in the desert,
Our Lord, not only with your bread,
But with your very presence.
Give us today our daily bread...
We need food and drink, Lord,
And we need you too.
Bread and wine and Jesus.
I am the bread of life,
come to me all you are hungry and thirsty...
Be with us this week, our precious Lord,
As we travel through the good times and bad.
The days and the nights. Please remind us
To continue to look to you for help,
Strength, provision and guidance.
In Jesus name, Amen

Exodus 16, Lamentations 3, Matthew 4, The Lord's Prayer and John 6

64. Nothing Off Limits

We can bring everything to God, nothing is off limits with Him.
Nothing too difficult, too harsh, too dark,
Nothing too strange, too frightening, too unexpected,
We can bring everything to God, nothing is off limits with Him.
Nothing too ordinary, too silly, too small,
Nothing too big, too overpowering, too strong,
We can bring everything to God, nothing is off limits with Him.
Nothing too ridiculous, too stupid, too embarrassing,
Nothing too serious, too irresponsible, too regrettable.
We can bring everything to God, nothing is off limits with Him.

Romans 8 vv 38-39

65. Psalm 1

1:1 Happy are those who do not follow the advice of the wicked, or take the path that sinners tread,
Those who choose another way, those who go against the popular flow.

1:2 Their delight is in the law of the Lord, and on his law they meditate day and night.
They carry the words of truth, light and hope within their being, a different text, a different way.

1:3 They are like trees planted by streams of water, which yield their fruit in its season, and their leaves do not wither.
The ways of their God bring life, strength and sustenance, living water refreshes them and those they meet.

1:4 The wicked are not so, but are like chaff that the wind drives away.
Though they appear to prosper now, their days are numbered, another day will dawn and it will not be theirs.

1:5 Therefore the wicked will not stand in the judgment, nor sinners in the congregation of the righteous;
Their power will be washed away like words etched in the sand, their dubious straw-clutching will be long-forgotten.

1:6 For the Lord watches over the way of the righteous, but the way of the wicked will perish.

Lord we long for this, for the day when your ways will fill the headlines, when despair, fear and cynicism will be shadows dispersed by the sun of that new morning.

66. Longings

We all have our longings O Lord,
And we bring them to you as part of our worship.
As Moses stood on that mountain top and looked down,
Saw the beauty of the Promised Land,
Longing to be there, longing to see the fulfilment of his dreams
And the end of his journey.
We all have our longings O Lord,
And we bring them to you as part of our worship.
As Moses spoke with you Lord,
Shared the closeness of friendship and trust
With you, the Living God,
The one who called him and have him a second chance.
We all have our longings O Lord,
And we bring them to you as part of our worship.
As we, like Moses, catch a glimpse of a better life,
A different world, full of changes for the good,
Longing to take our people there, all those we know and love,
To a place of hope and kindness, respect and freedom.
We all have our longings O Lord,
And we bring them to you as part of our worship.

Deuteronomy 34 vv 1-12

67. Paving the Way

When the people came to cross over the Jordan River, the priests stepped into the water first, carrying the ark, to pave the way for others to follow in their steps. As we reflect on this reading take a moment to look down at your own feet and to think about where you will be going in this coming week. Take a moment as we pray now, to remind yourself that God is with you in all situations.

Prayer:
Lord, you call us at times to step ahead of others,
Like those priests stepping into the River Jordan.
You ask us to pave a way, with our own footsteps,
And our own travelling,
To move with you, in your way, in your time.
Help us please, when that is not easy,
When we feel alone in our walking and travelling.
Help us to know that you tread the path with us,
And though we may be fearful
And our steps may be reluctant and faltering,
It is enough that we take one step at a time.
So Lord we commit this week to you,
And the places we will go,
Knowing that you understand and long to help us each day,
Wherever we may find ourselves.
In Jesus's name,
Amen.

Joshua 3 vv 7-17

68. Promises

34:1 Then Moses went up from the plains of Moab to Mount Nebo, to the top of Pisgah, and the Lord showed him the whole land. The Lord said to him, "This is the land of which I swore to Abraham, to Isaac, and to Jacob, I have let you see it with your eyes, but you shall not cross over there."

To stand like Moses, and see the promises of God,
To know the nearness of God, the friendship they shared,
To have travelled so far, come through so much,
To have a vision of freedom, and to pass it on to others.

There are times when, like Moses, we stand and look and
See more, see what no one else sees,
The promise, the vision of a better world, a better life,
Hope for others, a new way forward.

We long to pass on that vision as Moses to Joshua,
We see it for others, and hold it in our prayers.
That promise, that view of a better world, a better life,
And we long for its coming, for truth, hope and freedom.

69. I Am

I am the way, I am the truth, I am the life,
I am the resurrection.
I am a fresh start and a new beginning,
A voice in the wilderness and a light in the dark.
I am hope when all is lost,
I am understanding when others fail.
I am peace amidst the raging and the storm,
I am a single step when moving seems so hard.
I am the one who never leaves,
Never fears, never abandons, never gives up,
I keep believing when you cannot.
I know those doubts and questions,
Hurts and disappointments,
I carry them in my scarred hands,
And sacrificed body.
I am with you wherever you go.

70. Open Book

Sometimes we open the book,
Take a stroll through the pages,
Weave between the words,
Take the hand of one or two phrases,
And sidestep some of the others.
Sometimes we open the book,
And find ourselves mirrored in the truth and facts,
Led forward by the parables and poetry.
Our lives, our struggles, our hopes and tears,
Right there in the bursts of laughter,
The smiles of friendship,
The broken-hearts and the wandering ways.
Sometimes we open the book,
And the words leap off the page,
And hug themselves to the depths of our being.
Sometimes the sentences seem cold and hard,
Hanging there like sharp, jagged icicles,
Posing tough questions, staring at us, hands on hips.
Sometimes it shakes us by the shoulder,
Sometimes it whispers in our ear.
Sometimes we wrestle, winning as we lose,
Sometimes we see ourselves,
And are never quite the same again.
Some days we don't open the book,
And some days we do.
Some days it waits on the shelf, gathering dust,
And some days it bursts open,
Irrepressible,
Spilling meaning, comfort, questions and inspiration.

71. The Whisper

There is a whisper, a quiet call.
A still small voice,
Willing us to come out from life's crevices,
From the rocks we hide behind.
A subtle, hopeful invitation,
'Come out, please come and see me.
Show me your face,
Tell me your secrets.
Share your hopes and dreams,
Your fears and longings.
For I love to hear your voice,
And spend time with you.
There is a gentle, divine request,
A whisper, a quiet invitation,
Saying, 'Come out, let's talk,
Let's spend some time together,
For I delight in you
And love to see you.'

Song of Songs 2 v 14

72. Stumpery

I stroll through the stumpery and wonder.
It's like a valley of dry, dinosaur bones,
Splendid wreckage from the past, dead yet glorious,
Bulbous, jagged, sculpted pieces of shrapnel,
Severed from the living things they once held.
All crags and crannies and crooked corners,
A graveyard of wood and splinters and spiky claws.
The once-living now nothing more,
Or less, than staggering artworks,
To be studied, admired and marvelled at.
Once the vital, powerful means of life-support,
The vital foundations of colossal timber behemoths,
Now merely disconnected museum pieces,
Here for our wonder and reflection,
Magnificent, yet devoid of life.
This skeletal forest, no longer changing shape,
Trapped in its own contorted, sapless, weathered future.

Ezekiel 37

73. Single Moment

In any single moment...
One of us walks, one of us runs, many of us limp.
Some move forward, some slip back,
Some are stuck. Some are joyful, some are broken,
Some praise, some question,
Full of faith and doubts. In any single moment...
Some openly carry their need of God,
Some wonder if he is interested, some don't know.
Some feel the good weight of significance,
Some fear they are merely a smudge in history.
In any single moment...
Some press themselves into their sadness,
Some embrace the first glimmers of hope,
Some crack open the doors of their heart,
Some stand in fear, too brittle to do so.

74. Broken Praise

'I must speak because I am greatly disturbed…'
He pours out his heart, wrenches open his soul,
Spills his guts and empties his mind.
'I must speak because I am greatly disturbed…'
A man whose life lies in tatters around him,
He squats amongst the twisted wreckage,
The debris of his hopes and dreams and loves.
'I must speak because I am greatly disturbed…'
He sobs his message, tells it all to God.
A worship song written in sweat and blood,
Anger and pain punctuating the phrases.
'I must speak because I am greatly disturbed…'
And as he sings and keens and cries,
He finds another layer of faith,
Born of his troubles, shaped by his agonies.
'My Redeemer lives and I will see him…'
He gasps, 'Someone is still on my side.'
He sniffs, the grief smeared across his face,
He raises his eyes, scorched red with searing tears,
And lifts them to heaven.

Job 19

75. Searching

For thus says the Lord GOD: I myself will search for my sheep, and will seek them out.

I won't stay at a distance. I will come out into the world I made. Whatever the circumstances, whatever the weather.

For thus says the Lord GOD: I myself will search for my sheep, and will seek them out.

I will get my hands dirty; I'll search high and low. I won't leave my sheep abandoned and lost.

I will risk everything to find and feed them, even if it should cost me dearly. I will spend all my energy, all my time.

For thus says the Lord GOD: I myself will search for my sheep, and will seek them out.

Even if it takes me to death itself. I will cross that threshold, lay down my life, and surrender everything.

My sheep are precious to me, it breaks my heart to see them wandering and lost, without a shepherd.

For thus says the Lord GOD: I myself will search for my sheep, and will seek them out.

I know them all by name, and will continue searching for them.

To show them I care, to show them I understand, to show them I am on their side. I love them.

For thus says the Lord GOD: I myself will search for my sheep, and will seek them out.

76. Don't Stop

Don't stop believing...
Though you don't have all the answers,
Though you sometimes think you do.
Don't stop believing...
Though you feel like giving up,
Though you want to take a wrong turn.
Don't stop believing...
Though the tunnel seems endless,
And the light is slow in appearing.
Don't stop believing...
Though the days are long,
The nights are endless,
The pressures are great,
And the disappointments overshadow you.
Don't stop believing.
Please.
Because I never will.
In you.

77. Single Moment (2)

In any single moment
Some fill their pockets with generous kindness,
Some find nothing but dust and sand,
Some overflow with inspiration,
Some feel inspiration slipping away.
Some are wide-eyed and frightened,
Some are wide-eyed and confident.
Some plot evil, some are changing wrong to right.
So many of us living so many lives.
We bring this single moment to you,
And place it as an offering
On the altar of resurrection and crucifixion.

78. Present

I'm the nudge inside your conscience,
The anger you feel at injustice.
I'm the whisper in the night,
The push to keep on going,
The call to take another step.
That unexpected pat on the back,
That boot up the backside to spur you on.
I'm the beckoning that tugs at your soul,
The opening of your inner eyes.
The refocussing of your vision,
The unstopping of your ears.
The one who is always with you,
The one who is ever present,
The one who longs to know you better.

79. Sour Wine

Jesus drinks the sour wine of our shame;
Drinks deeply of it, drinks it down and absorbs it.
Mysterious and bitter, the poison that contaminates,
Seeps into our being and corrodes our
Gifts, our hope, our laughter and caring.
He drinks the sour wine, drains the cup,
And somewhere behind the pain and insults,
There's an echo of extraordinary words,
'If the son sets you free you shall be free indeed.'
He drinks the sour wine.
Willingly. For us.

Luke 23 vv 32-36

80. Carrying

We carry our burdens,
Our friends, enemies, achievements and failures,
Celebrations, frustrations and disappointments.
The steps we have taken, the ground we walk on,
The dust under our nails, the lines on our faces,
The aches and pains and bruises.
The things which make us laugh and cry,
The jokes, the comments, the silences, the shouting,
The money we spend and the clothes we wear.
We carry our doubts, our fears and wondering,
Our nightmares, and daydreams,
Our goals and aspirations.
We carry our history, and our tomorrows,
The known and the unknown,
The 'what was and what might just be'.
And we carry each other.

81. Salvation

Entertainment can't save us,
Shopping can't save us,
The adverts can't save us,
Movies can't save us,
Fashion can't save us,
Sport can't save us,
Box sets can't save us,
Politicians can't save us,
Money can't save us,
Sex can't save us,
Neither can power, looks or popularity.
Oh dear. How miserable is this?
Who can rescue us from our inevitable mess?
Thanks be to the One who made everything,
And to the One he sent,
Who turned up because we tried everything,
And nothing else could save us.
In Him we exist, in Him we are rescued,
In Him we begin again.

Romans 7

82. Carrying (2)

He carries that cross, hauls it up that hill,
The ills, pains, sorrows and scars,
Carries it to death.
Through every midnight, every final moment,
And on into every new dawn.
He carries the depth of understanding,
Of life in all its colours, the shades of our hurt,
And each bright, rising sunrise of hope.

He carries us,
When the burdens are too much,
When the weight overwhelms us.
He carries us,
Through the strength of others,
The words, actions, smiles and tears
Of those who listen, help, sit and stand
With us,
As we carry on.

83. Living Sacrifices

Our lives are this strange mixture -
Glory and grit,
Seeing and believing,
Questioning and doubting,
Loving and hating,
Getting it right, getting it wrong,
Regretting and remembering,
Trusting and fearing,
Judging and forgiving,
Warm hearts and cold,
Waiting and longing,
Complaining and celebrating,
Good Friday and Easter Sunday,
Christmas and Advent,
Wondering and hoping,
Peaceful and stressed.
Our lives are this strange, strange mixture,
Which you understand,
And we often don't.
And this is our worship,
We bring them today to you.

My sad life's dilapidated, a falling-down barn;
build me up again by your Word.
Barricade the road that goes Nowhere;
grace me with your clear revelation.
I choose the true road to Somewhere,
I post your road signs at every curve and corner.
I grasp and cling to whatever you tell me.
Psalm 119

84. No Longer

No longer a slave to fear
But still a servant to worry
No longer a slave to putting others down
But sometimes a servant to unfair criticism
No longer a slave to hating
But sometimes a servant to disliking
No longer a slave to rage
But sometimes a servant to unrighteous anger
No longer a slave to destruction
But sometimes a servant to tearing down
Rather than building up.

85. Longing

We long for you Lord,
Our prayers rise up,
Spoken and unspoken.

Like something broken longing to be mended,
Like bad news longing for good,
Like discordant noise longing for silence,
Like gnawing hunger longing to be fed.

We long for you Lord,
Our prayers rise up,
Spoken and unspoken.

Like a war zone longing for peace,
Like a bitter argument longing to be resolved,
Like a poisonous wound longing for healing,
Like a locked door longing for the key.

We long for you Lord,
Our prayers rise up,
Spoken and unspoken.

Like a question longing to be answered,
Like a puzzle longing to be solved,
Like the unloved longing for love,
Like the rejected longing for acceptance.

We long for you Lord,
Our prayers rise up,
Spoken and unspoken.

Like the powerless longing for justice,
Like the disappointed longing for another life,
Like the prodigal a long way from home,
Like the father waiting at the open gate.

We long for you Lord,
Our prayers rise up,
Spoken and unspoken.

86. We Wonder

As the sun disappears behind another night sky,
We wonder.
As the clouds swallow the light and steal it away,
We wonder.
As the darkness closes in, stealing evidence of the day,
We wonder.
Will it come back?
Will the sun rise again?
Will hope warm our hearts?
As Christmas clouds our vision,
As Advent seems a distant old fashioned memory,
In the bustle of the season and the rush of life,
We wonder.
Where is the child?
Will we find him again?
And does his growing up still change things?

87. Filled

Filled with God's spirit,
Fresh from the Jordan baptism,
You went O Lord –
Not to conquer nations
Or destroy evil;
But to a quiet place,
An empty place,
To prepare to serve the world.

Filled with God's spirit,
Fresh from the Jordan baptism,
You went O Lord –
Not to assert your authority
Or make yourself great;
But to be alone,
To face temptation,
To prepare to serve the world.

Filled with God's spirit,
Fresh from the Jordan baptism,
You went O Lord –
Not to draw up a 'to do list'
Or to network with the great and the good;
But to nurture humility,
To shun popularity,
To prepare to serve the world.

Filled with God's spirit,
Fresh from the Jordan baptism,
You went O Lord –

Not to practice impressive miracles
Or prepare impressive speeches;
But to spend time with your Father,
To listen to him,
To prepare to serve the world.

Mark 1 vv 9-13

88. Christmas Every Day

Shepherds and travellers continue to find him,
Angels keep on bringing the message,
In the day-to-day skies of life's broad canvass.
Stars show the way, burning dimly and brightly,
On our streets and screens.
And so many unlikely folks, and unexpected visitors,
Keep stumbling across the signposts,
And spotting the lights in life's sky.
And the child remains accessible and humble,
Right there for the weak and strong, rich and poor;
Sidestepping the spin, requiring no privilege,
Protected by no barriers or pomp.
And Christmas dawns again and again and again,
Not bound by calendars or seasons or holidays,
But a daily occurrence as chains break and eyes are opened.

89. Hallelujah, Amen

Is an Hallelujah any less
If we're murmuring or mumbling?
Is an Amen any less
If the words come stumbling?
Though it's hard to say, My Lord,
Though the praise is barely heard,
Though it's whispered in the dark,
Though the worshipper is crumbling...
'Hallelujah, Amen.'

'Hallelujah, Amen.'
We sacrifice these words again.
In true humanity we speak,
With our voices strong and weak;
Needing no pretence or fear,
As we praise the God who's near.
It's a cry, a gasp, a small hurray,
Expressing much we cannot say,
'Hallelujah, Amen.'

'Hallelujah, Amen.'
We say them once again,
More than words in the air,
Whether life feels wrong or fair.
With smiles, or frowns, or stares,
To the God who hears and cares.
We say it again,
'Hallelujah, Amen.
Hallelujah, Amen.
Hallelujah, Amen.'

90. Sandals

Lord, we approach with bare feet,
Vulnerable, humble, liberated.
Letting go of so much that might get in the way.
Aware of our own frailty, our humanity,
Sensing the heat of reality with each step.
We are not God and He is –
The one who calls us near.
Invites us to approach.
To listen, to grow, to change.
Beckoned by that distinct voice,
In the flames and the crackling.
So we approach with bare feet.
Daring to remove, just for a moment anyway,
The sandals of our small security.
Amen.

91. Save Us/Holy Ground

As we stroll, bumble and hurry
Through the land of our daily lives,
Doing the things we must do,
The things we choose to do,
The things we need to do;
Save us Lord from moving too fast
And missing those burning bushes.
Those moments when the sudden burst
Of your presence might take us by surprise,
In the ordinary things,
In those bushes that burn anyway,
In the heat of the day,
In the daily run of desert life.
Save us Lord from moving too fast
And missing those burning bushes.
Missing those small miracles,
Those whispers and nudges,
Those signs of your kingdom.
The reassurance that you are near to us,
That your presence is with us.
In the rushing and the strolling,
In the darkness and the dawn.
Save us Lord from moving too fast
And missing those burning bushes.

Exodus 3 vv 1-10

92. Colours and Portraits

At first the world was flooded
With the colours of rainbow,
Rampant, Uncontrollable, Exhilarating,
Then a kind of red-grey
Muddied the picture,
The colour of deceit and death.
Then a remix of the rainbow,
The colours less bright,
The hues merging,
But still an expression of the rainbow.
Then a deep, deep crimson,
A scarlet outpouring flooding life's screen,
Daubed with the strokes of a cruel cross.
And then the colours of dawn,
Bleeding across a new day,
But not from an open wound
From a healed one.
And then the whole palette
Was handed to the planet,
For people to pick up the brushes
And paint pictures themselves.
Not perfect works of art,
But a billion, billion tiny powerful
Portraits.

93. Daydream

I daydream on a street corner,
See the tide of people moving,
Ebbing and flowing.
And I dream of stardom,
And stories,
And heroism,
A right mix-up of aspirations
And fantastic things.
I dream of rescuing people,
Scooping lives out of this humdrum world,
Delivering them safely into the next.
A Narnia free of cynicism, malice and cold shoulders.
Of pulling them from the burning building of this world,
To the safe and peaceful confines of another.
And it will be years until
I see myself clearly enough to know
That I am not the hero to do that.
But I still dream,
I still wonder,
And I still watch the ebb and flow.

94. Not Me

If it had been me
There on that dark Friday,
With the words 'Father forgive them...'
Hanging in the air,
I might have been tempted to add,
'Well... apart from him... and her, especially her,
They always got me down.
And that lot with their annoying habits.
And the bunch over there I just don't understand.
And that lot I can't control.
And a few others besides...'
But it wasn't me
There on that dark Friday,
With the words 'Father forgive them...'
Hanging in the air.
It was someone else.

95. Blunders
Sometimes those blunders and regrets
Can settle in the quiet corners of our being,
Becoming dark creatures
That bare their teeth from time to time,
Frightening and subduing us.
We need a St George to conquer these dragons,
A tiny hero in disguise, lying there in December straw;
One with 3 scars and the slain corpse of despair in his arms.

96. Dry and Dusty

Our lives can sometimes feel dry and dusty,
Repetitive and lacking in direction,
Scattered across the barren valleys of this life.
We need the breath of your spirit, O Lord,
To blow across the bones
Of today and tomorrow and the days after that.
Help us to hear the voice of your prophets,
Those who will stand up and beckon your presence,
Amongst the empty voices that merely batter us with sound.
Please revive us, inspire us,
And show us what it means to stand together,
Not in our own strength or small might,
But by your Spirit,
And in your Son,
Through whom we ask this,
Amen

Ezekiel 37

97. An Advent Prayer

Lord, Christmas so clearly affects us,
The plans, presents, parties,
And preparations of all kinds.
It affects our resources, our time, our energy,
But what of Advent?
The promise of your arrival,
The promise of change,
The promise of a new future.
How can that affect us?
Our time and energy and resources.
How can that vision of you and your presence
Make a difference to today and tomorrow?
Lord, please help us; help us to find ways to rediscover
And earth the promises of your life breaking into ours.
Help us to be a little different,
Help us to reshape our week a little,
Because of this time of knowing
That you are on the way.
Each day, each hour, each minute.
Help us Lord, please, Amen.

98. Keeping Going

Lord so many have served you down the years -
Standing tall, taking risks, their heads above life's parapet.
Some trusted and saw miracles,
Some trusted and gave everything for you.
Moses, Gideon, Ruth, David, Esther, Samuel, Hannah,
And so many more.
Help us remember them when we struggle to keep going.

Lord so many have served you down the years -
And so many continue to serve you today,
Some seeing miracles, some giving everything for you.
Some we hear about, so many we'll never know.
Help us remember them when we struggle to keep going.

Lord so many have served you down the years -
They saw in part, as we do, catching divine glimpses.
Seeing the future as if through a dusty window.
They waited and prayed, as we all wait and pray,
For the peace, the harmony and the fulfilment of your kingdom.
Help us remember them when we struggle to keep going.

Lord so many have served you down the years -
Running the race that requires dedication, faith and courage.
Thank you for calling us to follow in their footsteps,
To run for the prize only found in you.
Help us remember them when we struggle to keep going.

99. Changing Professions

Started out as a humble carpenter-builder,
Fixing furniture and houses with his earthly dad.
Working with wood and stone,
Crafting something good from very little.
Ended up as a Sunday gardener,
Fixing eternal things with his heavenly father.
Working with people like us,
Crafting something precious from very little.

100. Christmas Presence

A spoken word, a tongue of fire,
A burning bush, a rock,
An anchor, a still small voice,
A wrestling figure, a living word,
A fourth figure in a furnace,
A vision, a shining figure,
A tiny baby, a curious child,
A dedicated carpenter,
A wilderness wanderer,
An engaging teacher,
A witty storyteller,
A compassionate friend,
A vine, a road, the bread of life,
A wrongly convicted man,
A broken hero,
A dying revolutionary,
Forgiving to the last,
A death-defying gardener,
An impossible, irrepressible God,
Trusting, accessible,
Forever reaching out,
The first, the last,
Eternal and close,
Understanding and kind,
Always with us.

101. New Year

Our Christmas journeys may be
Stressful and difficult and demanding,
Whether trekking to a far destination
Or simply making it through the season,
Taking tough steps among the glitter and tinsel.
The season can be a time of hard travelling.
Heavily pregnant and 100 miles
From Nazareth to Bethlehem;
Strange men bursting in on the intimacy of birth;
Dreams about treachery and terror;
The flight of 400 miles to another border.
Strangeness, pressure and trouble,
Amongst the stars and dreams, hope and angels.
We stand on the border of another year,
The journey may look oddly familiar
Or strange, unknown and epic.
But we are offered an understanding hand,
By one who has lived his own difficult days,
And carries a light for the path.

Printed in Poland
by Amazon Fulfillment
Poland Sp. z o.o., Wrocław